THE STORM

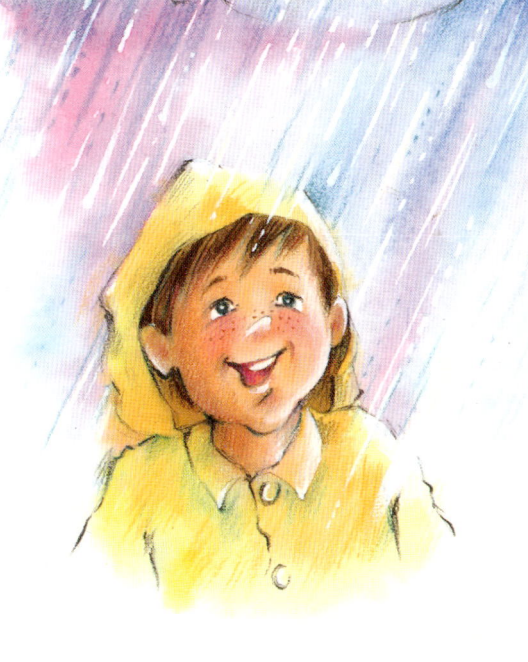

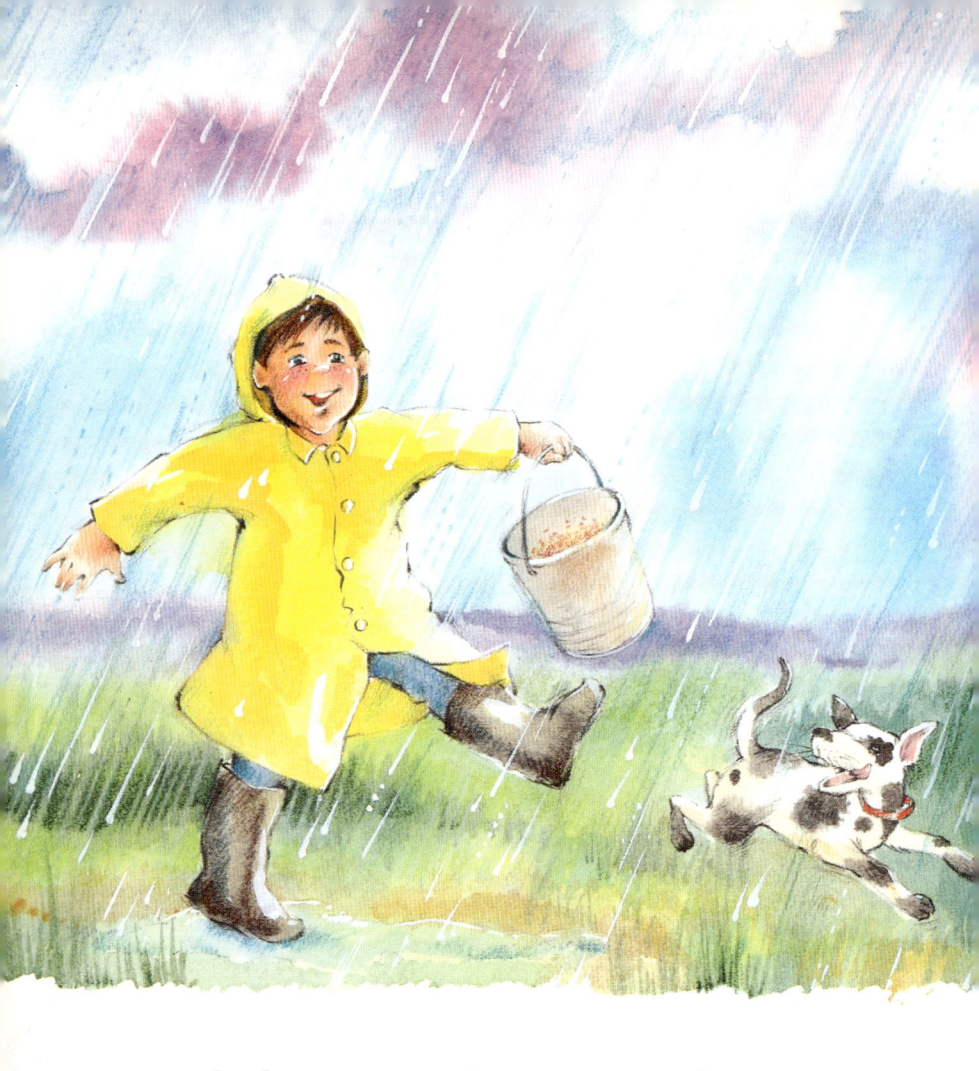

Splish go the raindrops.

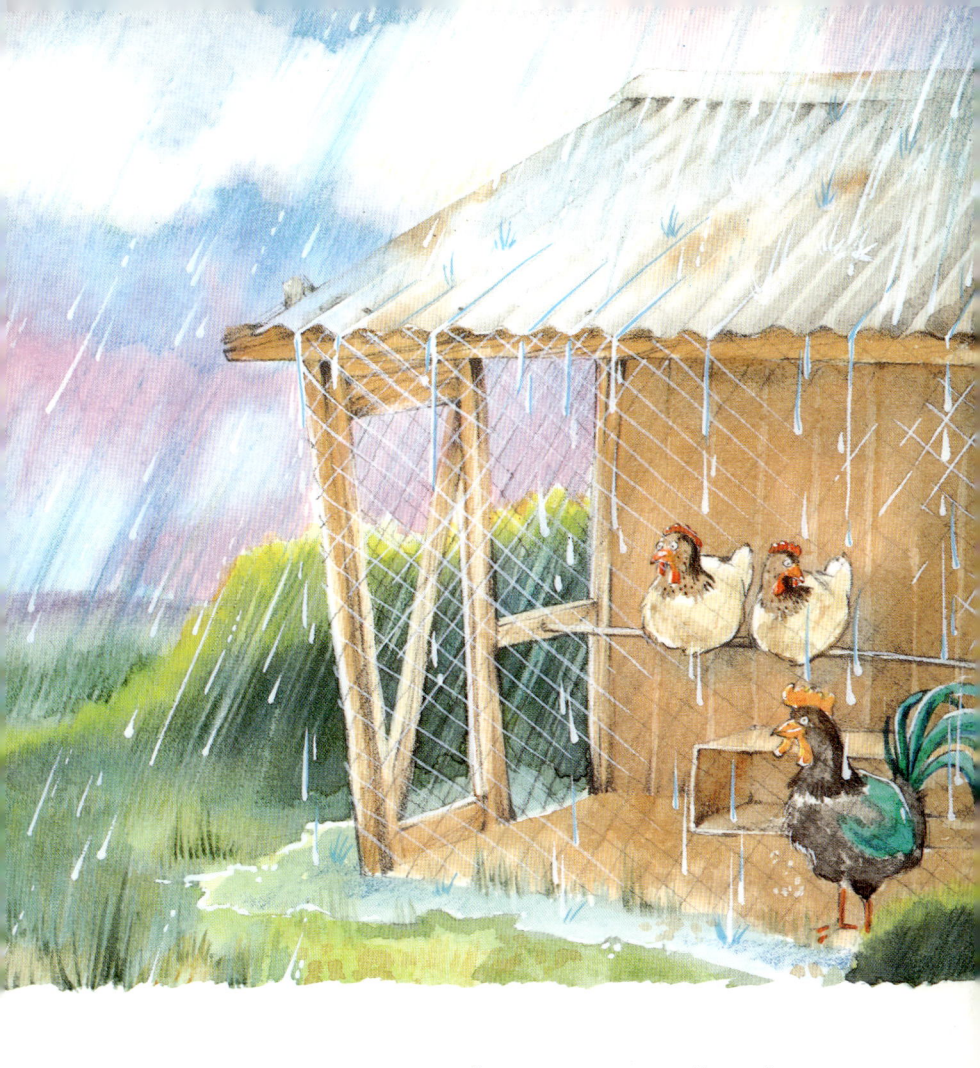

Listen to them *splash*.

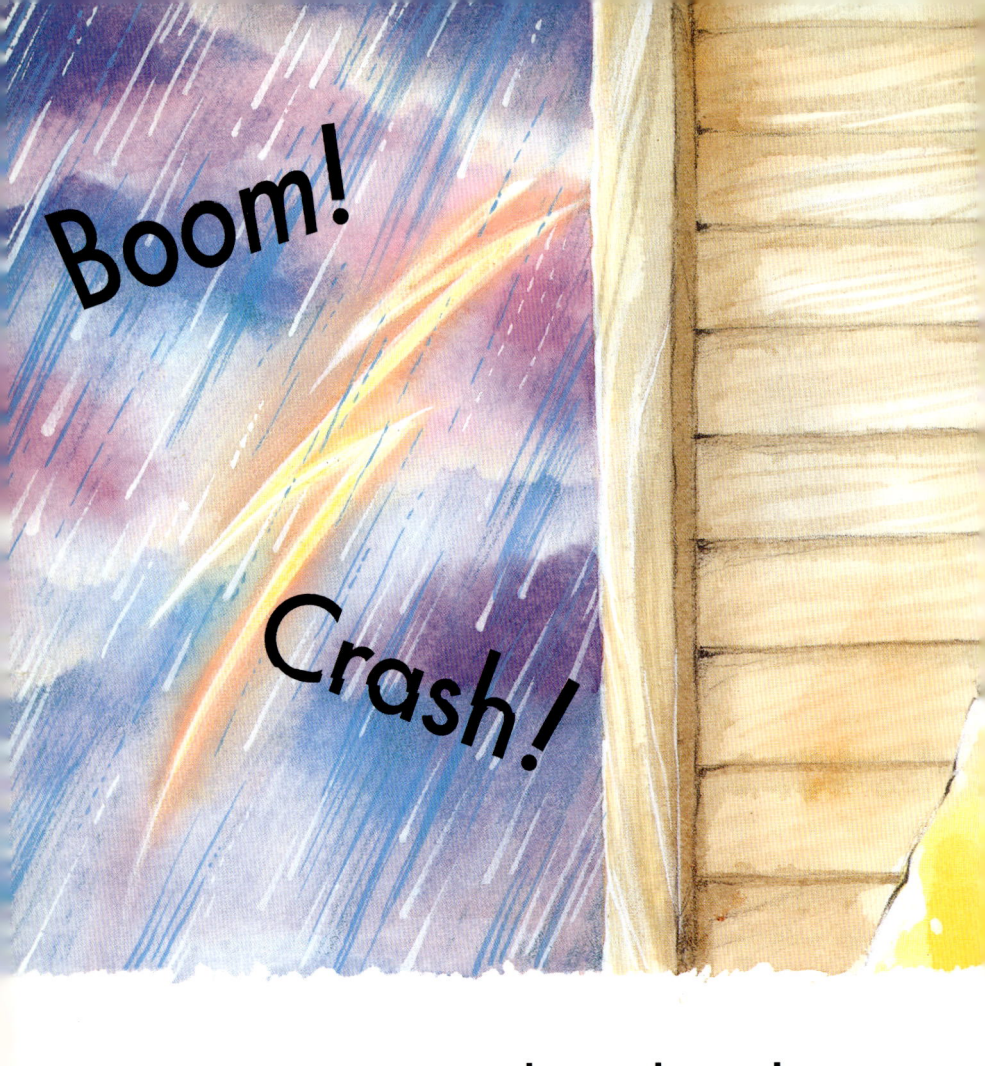

Boom goes the thunder.

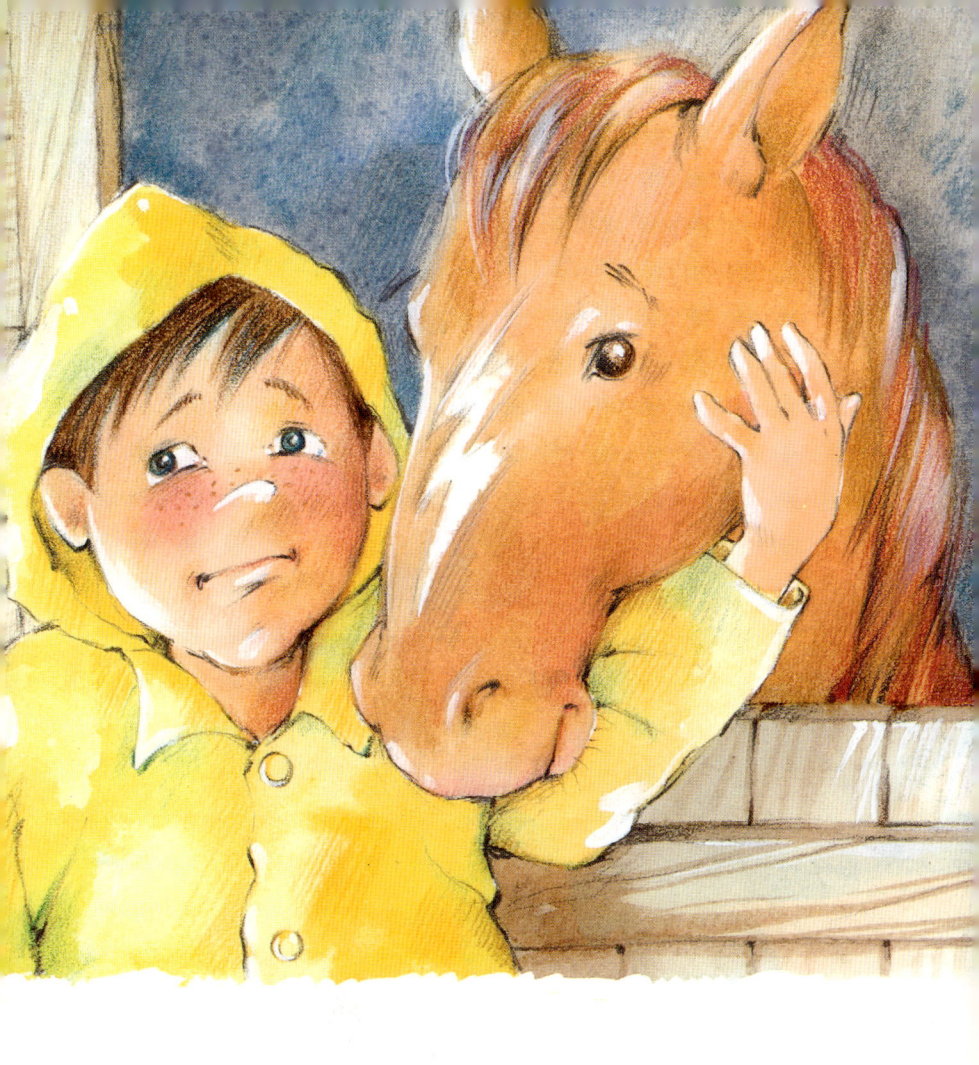

Listen to it *crash*.

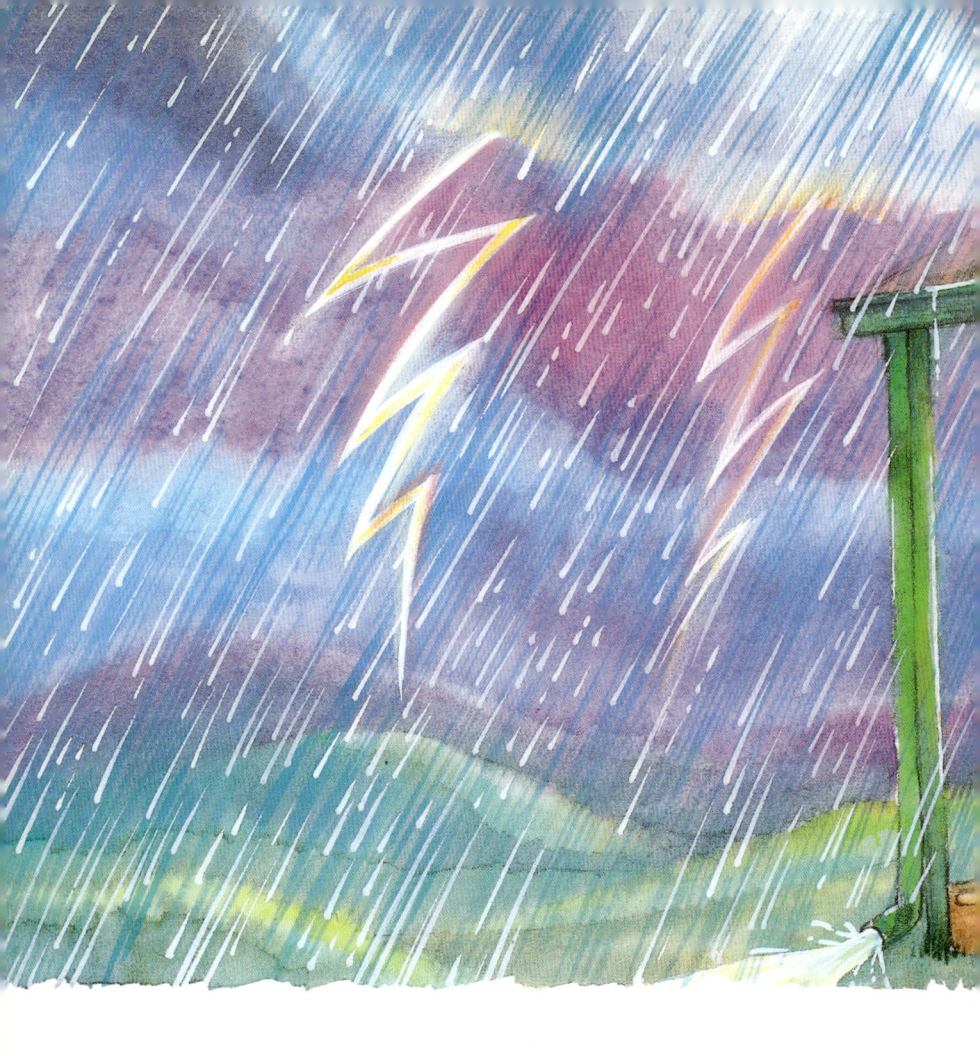

Splish! Splash! Boom! Crash!

6

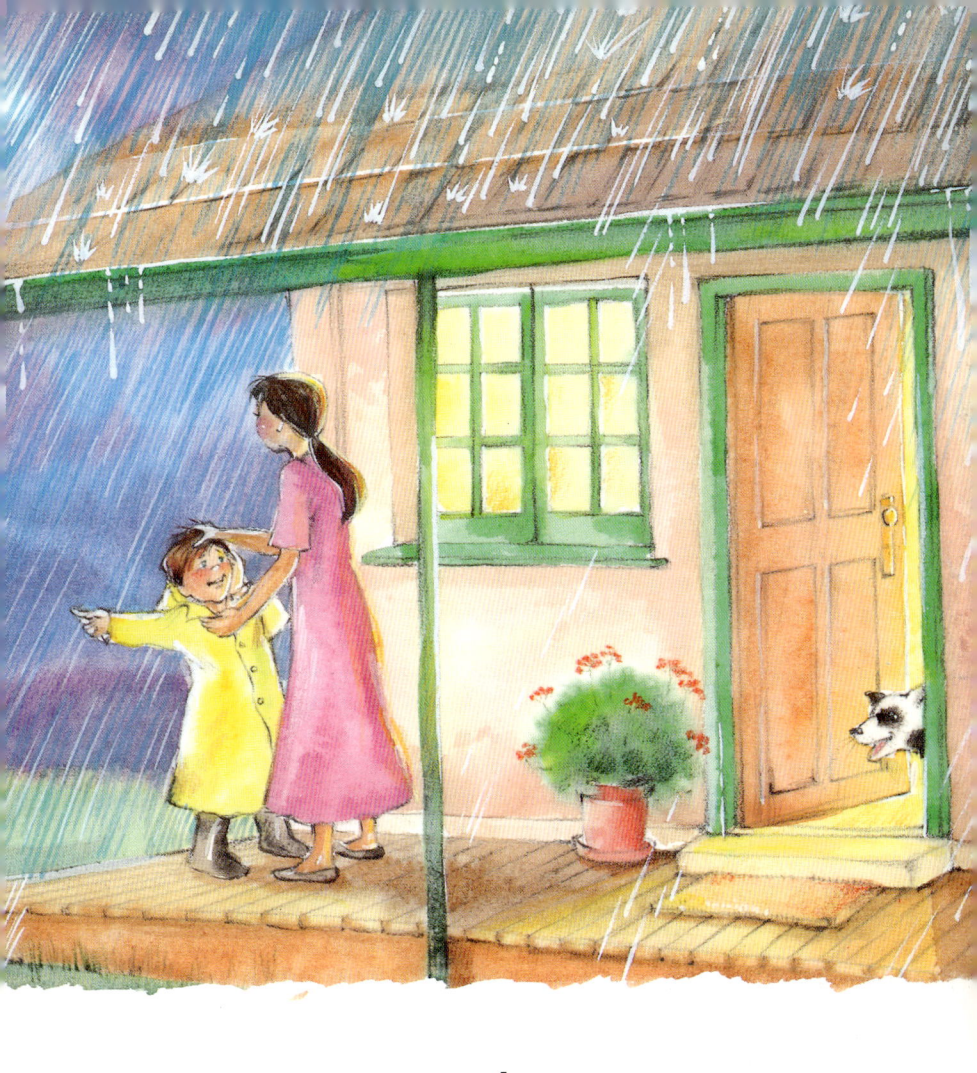

Listen to the storm.

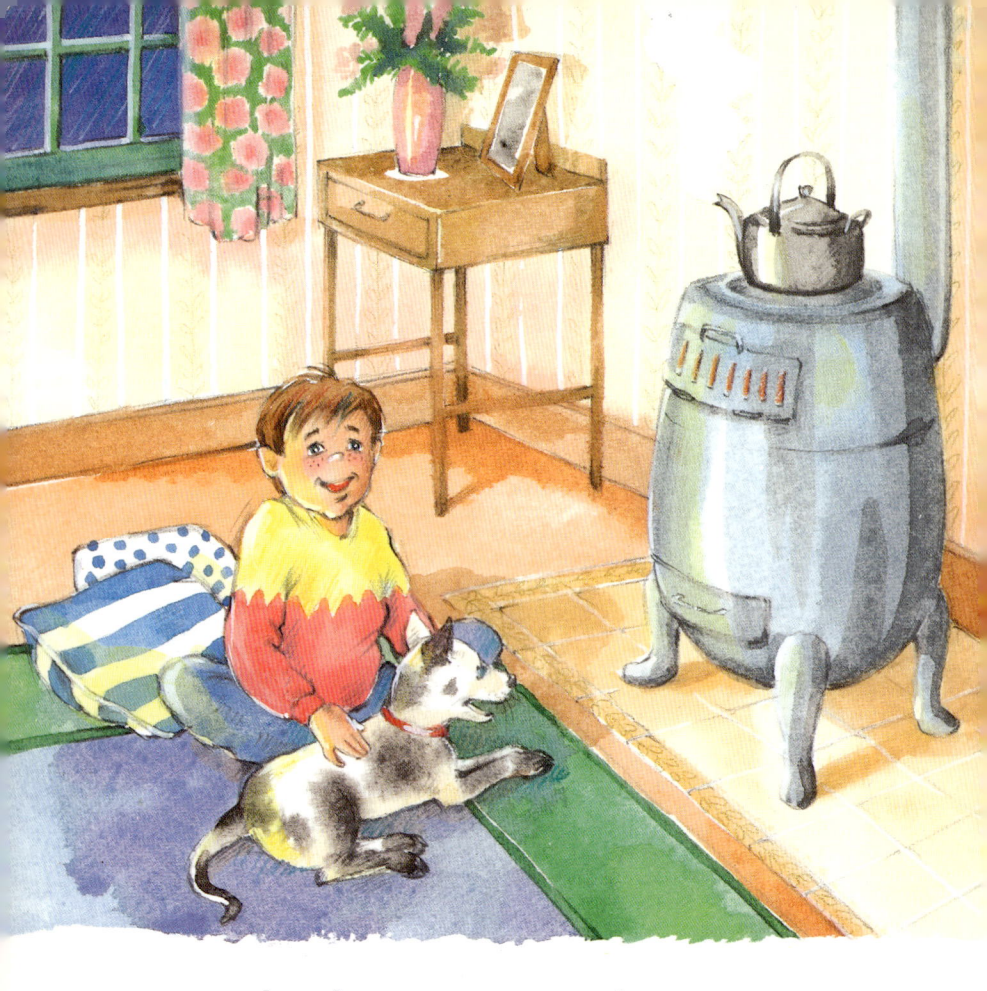

I'm glad I'm inside,
where it's snug and warm.